PRACTICAL APPROACHES
TO CHOOSING A CAREER

PRACTICAL APPROACHES TO CHOOSING A CAREER

DR OLUSHOLA ADEBORODE KOLAWOLE (MCIPS)

Contents

*This book is dedicated to my beloved late mother, **Mrs Agnes Modupe Kolawole (nee Ehindero)**, who despite her challenges as a widow, still supported my university education financially. Continue to rest in peace, Mummy, till we meet to part no more.*

Acknowledgements

Thanks to God Almighty for making this book a reality. I kept the manuscript for more than a decade, but now, it's a reality. All glory to Him.

Thanks to all who have impacted my career choice. To my beautiful friend, Oluwabukola Naiyeju, for holding my hand and encouraging me when the night was darkest and for allowing me to use your personal career story, thanks a bunch!

I appreciate Professor S.O. Owa of Landmark University, Nigeria, for accepting to write the Foreword. Also, to my brother Osee Amiolemen for your impact in my life while at the university, thanks a million.

I appreciate my friend Dr Sanfo Agyo for reading through the manuscript and for providing me with useful feedback. Special Thanks to Pastor and Pastor Mrs Isaac and Abiola Shofoluwe for the platform to serve God under you. To my Father in Lord, Prophet and Mummy Kehinde Ojo, thanks for your constant prayers and guidance. I want to thank Dr and Dr (Mrs) Femi and Rolake Fasae for your constant show of love.

I sincerely appreciate *The Roaring Writers Ng* for doing an amazing job of editing and proofreading the work. Very professional and amazing delivery.

I sincerely appreciate my friend, Dr Bola Oyelakin (Life Changers Network founder). Thanks for all your encouragement. You are one in a million.

Special thanks to my friends, Temitope Laniran PhD, Dimeji Sangodoyin PhD, Solomon Akopotozor PhD, Bakare Waheed PhD, Dare Ayoade (USA), Itoro Ekpo PhD, Destina Ovuakporie PhD, Adelowo Adesesan, Barrister Anthony, Seyi Ajayi, Bolaji Fashola. Thanks a million to Pastor Joseph Kolawole Ola for ensuring that this book got published. Thank you very much.

Thanks to all the parents, pupils, students, and staff of *The King's Palace Group of Schools* and those who have had an impact in the growth of the school since its inception, especially, Rev. (Dr) Olajide, Mr and Mrs Anthony Owolafe, Mr and Mrs Sanyaolu, Pastor Gbasinghan and many others — the list is endless. All I can say is thank you all.

To all those who have been supporting our vision and mission at the OAK Foundation, especially my SM Manager, Ehindero Damilola and Project Coordinator, Opeyemi Kolawole, and all our donors and partners, I say "thank you."

I cannot imagine the extent of work I would have to do without the support of Anuoluwapo, Oluwanifemi, Oluwadarasimi and Oluwadunsin. Thank you for all the patience, support and understanding.

Foreword

Many young men and women grope in the dark, not being able to tell what their careers would be. Many graduates move without perceiving which direction they are headed. Such are planktonic (floaters), tossed by every dictate of the day. When all class-mates talk about Medicine, they tilt that way, and if tomorrow it is Engineering, they follow suit. Such candidates end up settling for whatever comes up at the last minute.

It is better for a candidate to analyse himself/herself, what he/she is best at, and plan his/her life in the last line of best performance and interest. A good early discussion with a counsellor is very rewarding as it helps chart the route to the top. A very good practice is to be informed about career choices by reading a good book. This one you are holding is designed to assist in this crucial decision. It explains the practical approaches to choosing a career, guided by premises that analyse you and help you insist on the path to your career destiny.

I strongly recommend it for every young man and lady, early enough to help them form the right attitudes and self-analysis to be self-motivating to the top. Happy reading.

Rev. S.O Owa PhD, P.G.D.E
Professor of Applied Zoology
Landmark University
Omu-Aran, Nigeria

Introduction

Every person, at some point in their lives, has to
choose the career they would settle for in life. The
moment a young person starts to transit to higher
and more mature levels in life, they are confronted
with choosing that particular field that they find
themselves excelling at most. For instance, in my
country Nigeria, once a junior secondary school
student (the equivalent of year 7 and 8 in the UK) is
about getting into senior secondary school, the
teenager, his or her parents or guardian(s), and
teachers (or school counsellors, if any) begin to
select the subjects in which he or she performs
better than others and also scrutinise his or her
strengths generally. By doing that, they would be
able to determine whether science class, art class, or

commercial class is what is befitting for the child in senior secondary school.

Adults also come to points where they take decisions on what to settle for concerning their career; however, this little book shall focus more on 'career as it affects young people' more often than not and guide you on the path to choosing yours. The young person needs to understand what career is all about before delving into deeper discussions on the subject.

Most examples and illustrations will be given using the Nigerian setting to explain certain points. But do not worry if you are a non-Nigerian reading this; every illustration is self-explanatory, and you can easily substitute the setting with yours for better understanding.

Do read this book with an open mind and have personal reflections. Share with friends too, especially the young.

ONE

Understanding Career

F irst, let me tell you my personal story.

I remember when I was growing up, my heart desire was to become a chartered accountant and at the same time, an economist. I did not want to become a chartered accountant because I had a passion for it. It was because of influences from friends and colleagues in secondary school. We were told there was more money in the accounting profession, so, my choice of career shifted to that due to peer pressure. As time went on, there were other professions we were told made even more money. I found myself shifting from one to another with my friends. It was all about the money and not the passion. Whichever would make us richer was what we felt was best to settle for. There was no proper indoctrination either from parents, teachers or school counsellors on how to choose a career. We just kept shifting focus without a guide.

Due to this lack of understanding, upon admission into the tertiary institution for my first degree, I took up a course—Economics precisely, without any passion for it. I wanted to have an Economics degree and have an ICAN certificate at the same time. I was told that combining Economics and ICAN will give me a good boost. Unfortunately, it turned out to be a struggle and by 200 level (Year 2 at the University), I became eager to quit the course. I couldn't even envisage the possibility of an ICAN certificate anymore, so my dream of being an accountant was dashed. However, I became a graduate of Economics at the end of the four-year study.

My career path changed when I had the opportunity to travel overseas to undertake my Master's study. I chose my passion this time. I'm an organiser and seasoned administrator. I have always had a passion for these. Before choosing the postgraduate programme to settle for, I embarked on a search for the disciplines that would equip me with these skills formally. I found and settled for Logistics and Supply Chain Management. Every organisation needs this, especially where you have to organise activities and make them perfect for it. As opposed to my performance in Economics in my undergraduate days, I excelled in Logistics and Supply Chain Management, and immediately I finished, I got a job with the African Union Commission where I became the head of logistics of the arm where I served. I was happy on the job and it proved that I had, indeed, pursued my passion.

After that, I went for a PhD in the same course, and today, I'm having fun as I watch myself advance in my career. So, I forfeited my aim of becoming an accountant because that was not my passion. Although it seemed like I was a bit late in choosing the right path, I'm glad I was better late than never and I feel fulfilled every day of my life.

It is pertinent to understand the career concept vividly before delving into other aspects of it. Let's take a look.

What is a career?

Oxford Advanced Learner's Dictionary defines a career as "the series of jobs that a person has in a particular area of work, usually involving more responsibilities as time passes." Another definition of career is taken from the Longman Dictionary of Contemporary English: a job or profession for which one is trained and which one intends to follow for the whole of one's life. Career can as well be seen as a profession you are undertaking currently and/or you intend to undertake for the rest of your life. Take note, however, that some careers are legitimate while some are not. Armed robbery and smuggling are examples of illegitimate jobs. On the other hand, teaching, legal practice, medical practice, trading and photography are examples of legitimate jobs.

In choosing a career, you have to be very careful to avoid making mistakes. Any mistake made in choosing a career may be difficult to change in the future. For instance, if you decide in error to study and practice Medicine instead of Accounting in which you are gifted, when the error is discovered later, it will be difficult to switch back to Accounting. This is because it will entail writing Senior Secondary Certificate Examination (S.S.C.E), for the Nigerian setting, to obtain credit in the required commercial subject, and write University Matriculation Exams for entrance into the university to start from year one again. Though in the United Kingdom, you might opt for a top up course to change your career or apprenticeship so as to be skillful in the new career choice. However, it requires that you start all over. This is why one needs to be sensitive enough to know the God-chosen career for his or her life.

Many young people have failed in choosing the right career and today they are not happy with themselves. Indeed they are regretting. Some people choose careers for others forgetting that those who practice such are different individuals with their peculiarities. However, note that sometimes, the job you do to earn a living does not necessarily mean it is your career path. Many people in a country like the UK, USA and the likes are working in careers that are not their choices. They are doing it to pay their bills and take care of their families but it does not mean they want to make a future out of it. Therefore, there is a difference between a job you are doing and a job you want to make a career out of. I studied Economics in my first degree but today I am not working as an economist. I have a different career to that of an economist. So, sometimes, what you studied at the university level is not necessarily what you will follow for the rest of your life. I have seen some medical doctors who now take up politics as their full time career.

The place of counselling in the choice of a career is very important because the counsellors normally pay attention to the personal abilities of the person to be counselled.

Pause right now and reflect on these tips below.

Tips on career

- Identify and understand what you want and why you want it.
- Stand your ground on your ambition; do not allow anybody to dictate for you (but seek good counsel).

- Pursue your ambition with full determination. Never succumb to disillusionment.
- Do it with all your heart: devote your time and energy to it.
- Trust in God and fear Him.

In the succeeding chapters, we shall discuss vital steps to choosing a career detailed. In other words, what you are to check within you to determine the career path to follow.

TWO

Ability Check

Photo by Dragos Gontariu on Unsplash

V arious steps can guide one in choosing his or her career. It is important that we carefully follow the necessary steps in our career choices.

From this chapter, we will be looking at these various steps. The first is ABILITY.

A young boy of about 15 years in Senior Secondary School 2 (SS2) (the equivalent of year 11 in the UK) was called by a teacher to solve a problem in Mathematics for SS3 students (the equivalent of Year 12 in the UK). The boy heeded the teacher's call and he solved the question correctly. The teacher was greatly impressed and said to the class, "I knew he could solve the equation correctly, regardless of his class. He has the ABILITY to do it. Good boy!" She added. Also, a young boy of about 16 years was asked by his father to help pick up a heavy bag of about 60 kg which he did effortlessly. The Father exclaimed, "I knew he was going to carry it because I knew his ABILITY!"

This shows how important ability is in carrying out any task or in choosing a career.

Meaning of Ability

Ability is the power to do something. Therefore, in choosing a career you must know your ability, especially your intellectual capability. Many undergraduates of today are struggling with the courses they are studying. This is because they cannot cope with the demands of such courses. Some of them had thought they could do it because others were also doing it without knowing that the ability of A is different from that of B.

Some young people know in themselves that they cannot work as medical doctors because of fear of performing surgical operations, allergy to blood, etc., yet, because their friends have chosen such a discipline or because of parental influence, they go for it too. They fail to take cognisance of their ability.

More so, each profession or course has its peculiar demand. It is important to know your intellectual quotient or capability before choosing a course. For instance, in the example above, Medicine is not merely theoretical; in fact, it is more of practical--rigorous training involved. Therefore, to choose such a discipline, you must be prepared for the tasks.

Some students, for example, who were in commercial class in Senior Secondary school, knew that they were weak in Mathematics and calculations in general. Some hated it, actually, but because they considered Economics or accounting as a lucrative career, they opted for it, only to be struggling in the university because their choice also involved calculations which they hated while in secondary school. Many of them kept grappling with one failure or the other in the university. In most cases, they managed to graduate with poor grades. This is due to failure on their part to consider their endowments and abilities in choosing their career. Some people cannot deliver a speech in the public; they cannot even address two to three persons, yet, they are working in the teaching profession with their poor communication and interaction skills. They only succeed in being inefficient teachers. It is paramount that you know your ability.

Ability is innate, and by innate, it means something of natural expression in a person. He or she finds ease in that expression where others are struggling. For instance, when we are born, without a formal learning environment, we already start to speak our mother tongue. But when it comes to a second language, we need to acquire proficiency in a classroom setting to excel at it. So also, we should settle for that skill, job, discipline, etc., in which we find our innate ability. There's no way you wouldn't be efficient in it. It would not be rigorous, or tedious or burdensome for you. While others are worried about the tacky nature of the job, you would find fun in doing the job instead.

People who have become victims of wrong career choices end up with regrets. They are rarely happy about any aspect of the job. They only endure the job to earn a living. The reverse would be the case with you if you choose the right career.

Hazards and unfriendly circumstances could get people bored and tired as regards their job. This is more intensified when you choose a career that does not match your ability. Contrarily, you would soar in your career with intrinsic satisfaction welling up from your inside when you correctly choose that which suits your ability.

Why you need to choose a job or skill according to your ability

- You will be able to perform well in that career.
- You will be happier doing that job.
- You will have intrinsic and lasting satisfaction.
- The job will be very easy for you to carry out.
- Ultimately, as you do well in your career because you have the ability, you would

climb up the success ladder faster, that is, you would be successful.

Determinant questions

Ask yourself the following questions to identify your ability:

- What can I do best?
- Do I have the power to do it?
- Are my parents/guardians capable of sponsoring me?
- Do I have a means of sponsoring myself, that is, working and studying where there are no sponsors?

THREE

Talent Check

Photo by John Hult on Unsplash

Your talent enables you to prosper in your chosen career. Possession of talent is another requirement in choosing a career. Talent comes from God. This is why it is defined as your *unique endowment*. It can also be seen as *a natural ability to do something very well*. Do not forget the meaning of Ability. Talent is always God-given. It is in-born; it is not man-made. It is a gift from God. So, you need to discover your God-given talent(s).

Choosing a career for which you have the talent(s) will help you a lot. It will make you do well in your profession and promote your joy in doing such jobs.

Some people can do better in other creative works, such as informal types of jobs, than tasking their brains to study books (formal education). This refers to a situation, for instance, where someone can make use of the hands to design artistic works or being an artisan generally, which can fetch him a lot of money, yet, he is 'over-working' his brain in getting a formal education; reading "big books" to discover facts and understand the facts clearly.

Practical Examples of Talent

There was a friend of mine who studied Economics with me while at the university. He is very good at repairing faulty electronics (radio, television and others) without having learnt it from anybody. This is an example of the talent we are talking about; ability to do what others cannot do or ability to seamlessly do what others find a task to do.

To better understand the word talent and ability, read a fragment of my experience as a teacher below:

Some time ago, before I gained admission into the university, I was involved in teaching and I had a student whose name was Yemi. Yemi was very good at drawing but he was very dull academically. One day, his parents came to the school to report to me that their son (who at this point was already in was in SSS2; equivalent of Year 12 student in the UK) called them about three days ago at that time, saying that he was no longer interested in furthering his education, but that he would like them to allow him to focus solely on ARTWORK. He argued that what he needed to know are: how to write, read and speak English and he had already known them. I called Yemi later and asked him some questions. He answered me very well and I discovered that the boy will be better in using his hands than struggling with academics. Many of the young people of today need to discover themselves rather than merely struggling with academics.

Nevertheless, I advised him to give more time to his academic work to balance both as a sound academic background would enhance his artwork. Though, as it is now in the world, there is almost nothing you can do without being educated, else, your mates who are educated would surpass you. That is not to say that the purpose of being educated is for competing with your peers. No. It's to enhance your mind, understanding, career, and ultimately, your future. Yemi accepted my advice and continued with his academics while being an apprentice under a skilled artisan after school hours. This has helped Yemi to become one of the best artisans in his area.

Studying and developing your other skills is very possible. You can do both at the same time. This helps you to achieve your aim in life.

Positive Steps

- Let the talent(s) you possess serve as a guide in choosing your career.
- Mark out plans and step-by-step approaches in achieving your goal.
- Carry out your plans step-by-step.
- Be confident in every action you take.

However, do not neglect this:

It is good to have a basic education in today's fast-moving world to be able to rank among great men and women.

A wise person once said:

> *It is better you live in your talent than be a fool in someone else's talent.*

Anonymous

Ability + Talent + Right Choice = Excellence

FOUR

Interest Check

Photo by Element5 Digital on Unsplash

D ear reader, hope you are following the steps we
have discussed so far? Can you mention the

first two steps? Pause and mention them. I trust you got it right. Now, on to the third check: INTEREST.

Interest refers to delight, enthusiasm or self-motivation towards doing something or achieving a goal. It is the love you readily show towards an activity, a game, a career, an adventure, and so on. Some people take interest in listening to music, singing, watching and/or playing football, reading, drawing, teaching, etc. Interest in one's area of talent is very important in a life career. If you do not show interest in it, your talent cannot be developed.

Dear reader, if you do not have an interest in the course you are studying, you better develop an interest in it now so that you will be able to perform better in it. The story of Yemi in chapter three teaches us to first discover our talent(s) and ability as that will help you to develop your interest.

Your joy is fulfilled by doing what you give attention to most—what 'catches your fancy with ease'. Many people fail today because of lack of interest in their career. This is more rampant with those upon whom careers were imposed by either their parents, guardian(s) or by circumstances such as lack of money to further their education.

Here's a story to further buttress the point on Interest.

A medical doctor, during his convocation, handed over his certificate to his parents. He told the parents that the certificate belongs to them and not to him because studying Medicine was their idea, not his. He was more interested in being a sculptor. Sculpting had always caught his fancy but his parents saw no future in it.

So, handing the certificate over to them, he said, "Mom, Dad, here. I bagged it for you, to make you happy because that's what you want. Now, I'm ready to chase my happiness and pursue my sculpting dreams. I'm sorry if it disappoints you." He did not practice what he studied in school and he is enjoying his life as a sculptor today.

I remember a friend's career choice story, being influenced by her mother. She had always wanted to be a pharmacist, hence, her choice to be in science class. Her father approved of her decision and already enrolled her for private tutoring, preparing her for the science subjects. All her long vacation in-between resumption into a fresh admission/promotional class was used in studying those subjects with heaps of relevant textbooks just to ease the journey ahead upon resumption.

Unfortunately, her mother wasn't having it with her choice of career path. She wanted her to study Accounting. She was able to convince the daughter using her influence as a mother on her. My friend succumbed to her will which was majorly hung on admission and employment tussles. In her mother's exact words, "Everybody needs the service of an Accountant. You will be easily employable." She left science class after the first test assessment had been done in school, with her mum's words ringing in her head and settled for commercial class. She got the tag "Run away scientist" but it was not for no long, as she made remarkable strides in her new class. Her father was indifferent and assisted her with all the necessary support to get her acquainted with her new path. Today, she's a proud Chartered Accountant, having graduated from the university as one of the best female Accounting department graduating students and she currently has many professional qualifications to her credit.

While her childhood passion had always been to be a Pharmacist, she can't stop talking about her story of how she made a U-turn in her choice of career and how successful she is now.

Today, I can boldly say my friend found fulfilment, pride and joy in the Accountancy field. She is one of the most successful and brilliant accountants I have seen. She got her Chartered status at a very young age and till now, she hasn't stopped learning and achieving greater feats.

The line to note in this story is that, because it worked for this my friend does not mean it can work for everybody. We need to understand the need for personal interest, personal conviction and passion. Although my friend was pushed to become an accountant, she was convinced about her new future path, so she developed interest laced with passion for excellence. Without all these, she possibly wouldn't have been as successful as she is today.

Another parental influence was seen in a story of a young girl, whose dream was to become a Neurosurgeon. It had always been her dear dream to become a surgeon with impact. She had already made plans to be in science class to achieve this, but her mother, who thought scientists' dreams to be most times unrealistic, insisted on commercial class for her.

Her argument was based on the fact that a good number of people that had the same aspiration to become either a medical doctor, surgeon, e.t.c., usually ended up changing their courses at university level due to high admission requirements and other factors. According to her, many times, those people out of frustration end up in other professions, taking any science course thrown at them. Ultimately, the goal of being a medical doctor or surgeon is shattered. They later on find other professions upon graduation, thereby, rerouting unnecessarily after passing the rigours of learning science courses. She simply considered the commercial class career path as easier and more realistic.

She also buttressed on the number of years she would spend in training to become a surgeon and the resources. She later opted for commercial class regardless of her passion.

Parental guidance is good but over influencing a child's choice of career path is detrimental and destructive to the child's future. Let every child find their passion, fulfil their aspirations and let them pursue their personal goals. Parents should be mindful while guiding so as not to impose their own selfish parental aspirations on their wards/children.

Parents/guardians/teachers, do not impose your own career choices on your children/wards/students. Rather, allow them to choose what they want for themselves. Your duty is to guide them and not to dictate for them and if you must dictate because you have seen the future environment ahead of time, do it convincingly and in prayer to God.

FIVE

Now, Start Studying!

Photo by Eliott Reyna on Unsplash

After identifying your ability, talent, and interest, the next step to take is to STUDY.

It's time to be a master in your craft, on the job, in your career, etc. The story of Yemi in chapter three is a practical example. He both studied in secondary school (formal education) and he was allowed to be an artisan (informal education) through an apprenticeship in a private established institution.

The Dictionary of Contemporary English (Third Edition) says that to study is 'to spend time reading, going to classes, etc., to learn about a subject.' It could also be seen as the activity in which one engages himself/herself to acquire knowledge or skill about a particular course or subject of interest.

The most common way in which people build their knowledge or skill is by having a formal education in a classroom setting which is fine. However, as the world advances, newer learning environments are being explored. The classroom setting provides you with the basic education you need to navigate the world of your ability and interest in general, but when you want to go professional or be a reference point in that field, you have to look beyond classroom formal education as it is highly limited.

By regular classroom learning (having rounded off your secondary school education), using the

Nigerian education standard as an illustration, we mean institutions such as government-owned or private universities, government-owned or private polytechnics, colleges of education, etc. Here, you can major in your field of interest, but it is important that afterwards or while studying, you attend professional training centres, and undertake apprenticeship if you have hands-on skills. For those with hands-on skills, attending monotechnic is also highly recommended. A monotechnic is a tertiary institution that provides instruction in a particular field (technical subject). That is, it is the smallest type of tertiary institution that focuses on training students in a single subject. An example of a monotechnic is the National Institute of Information Technology (NIIT) where students get first-hand training and skills in computer software. The kind of knowledge and skill gained here is way above what the polytechnics and universities will impart in you.

In modern times, you can now take online classes, tutorials, trainings, seminars, and conferences to build your knowledge and skill. These online platforms can be via general online learning platforms like Udemy, Future Learn, SkillShare, Go Skills, Coursera, EDX, etc.; online university platforms that offer convenient courses, Whatsapp or Telegram classes (which are very short and have a lot of limitations but are still effective to some extent), Zoom classes, and many more. The list is endless in this digital age. Just keep exploring the net until you find the one(s) that suit your preference.

Studying will help you to know better and be well equipped in that course/job you have chosen.

Note, however, that studying does not exclude those with special needs and abilities. They are encouraged to study too, based on their talents and interests to develop expertise. We live in a world of endless possibilities these days. A perfect example is Haben Girma, the Eritrean Refugee who, though deaf and blind, pressed for her law dreams and, today is Harvard Law's first deafblind graduate. For more information on this, you can order her book, **Haben: The Deafblind Woman Who Conquered Harvard Law** via Amazon.

Positive Steps

- Once more, ensure you have the ability, talent and interest in your chosen career.
- Study to be well equipped for your career.

- Practice what you have studied well.

Results to Expect

- You will become a master in that field.
- It will qualify you to train/teach others.
- You will be admired and respected for your expertise.

SIX

Establish a Career Goal

Photo by Markus Winkler on Unsplash

"Life without a goal is like entering a gold mine and coming out with empty hands." — Japanese proverb

D ear reader, establishing a goal concerning your chosen course of study or desired career is the most important step in choosing a career. If you do not want to settle for failure in life, then you must set achievable GOALS for yourself.

What is a goal?

Some people call it AIM or a sense of direction. A goal is an aim, a purpose, an objective that is to be achieved. It is achieved by devoting the necessary interest, energy and resources to it in a timely and appropriate manner. After determining a goal (that is an endpoint), in setting goals and planning, ask yourself the following questions:

1. What do I want to achieve or become in life (i.e your goal)?
2. What would I do to be able to achieve or become it?
3. What do I need to achieve or become it?
4. Where do I start?
5. How do I start?
6. When should I start?

Setting a goal is essential to achieving what we want in life. What is important is where you are going, not necessarily where you are coming from. Many are failing today because they refused to set goals for themselves, or because they refused planning effectively how to achieve those goals.

How Do We Set Goals?

"Nothing is more terrible than activity without insight."

Thomas Carlyle (1795-1881)

First, let us look at types of goals in terms of duration (i.e, time).

There Are Three Kinds of Goals

1. Immediate Goals: These are goals/objectives/purposes you want to accomplish now, today, this week or a few months to come. For instance, you may want to attend a career seminar just for one day where you will be taught some skills that

you need in your career. This is an immediate goal.

2. Short term goals: These are goals that are achievable in calendar months. A desire to become computer literate by attending training programs just for 3 months is an example of short-term goals.

3. Long term goals: This takes more than 12 calendar months to accomplish. Undertaking a course in the university, College of Education, polytechnic, or apprenticeship also falls in this category.

Steps in Setting a Goal

1. Ensure your mind is at rest (it is better if you are alone). Then, write down what you want to achieve with your career (i.e your goal). For example, if you want to be a medical doctor, your goal may be to help sick people.

2. Determine what you need to achieve your career. Decide on the course to read and the basic admission requirement (i.e, the type of the subject you must offer and pass at the secondary school level; the subjects you must pass in the matriculation examination

and so on). Decide on the tertiary institution you want to attend. **Note:** make sure you find out from the brochure that the tertiary institution you choose offers the course you want to study.

3. Place the goal which you wrote in STEP 1 in a location where you can always see it to motivate you to always work towards it.

4. From time to time, find out where you are truly working towards achieving your career (to achieve its goal)

5. Your goal should sufficiently motivate you to pursue your career and achieve it.

6. Set a target time for achieving your career; this will further help you to work towards it.

7. You must be committed to your career/goal, otherwise, you will not achieve it.

The Experiences of People Who Have Goals in Life

- They have a sense of direction; they know where they are going.
- They are happy in life. You would want to be around them.
- They just keep working towards goals.
- They are self-motivated always; hardly ever

quitting a project. They ask, "Why do I have to quit?" not "When do I quit?"

- People with goals believe in themselves. It is better to try and fail than not try at all.

I encourage you, my dear reader, to set goals; do not waste your precious life.

The Experiences of People Who Live Life Without Goals

- Frustration: They are always frustrated about life. Of course, when you aim at nothing, you get nothing, and when you get nothing, you are frustrated.
- Unhappiness: Just like frustration, since goal-less people get nothing, they often end up unhappy. They keep blaming others for their predicament, poverty, illiteracy and so on.
- Having a bad character: Most young people who face life without goals end up wasting their lives among the gossips, hooligans, prostitutes, drug addicts and so on. Of course, evil communication corrupts (I Cor 15: 13). As such they imbibe bad character.
- Poverty: Young people who fail to choose the

right career and as well, fail to set goals to achieve in and through the career, turn out to be career-less, jobless and money-less. They become soaked with poverty. Although they may indulge in petty trade or as the Nigerian parlance puts it, 'bus-conductor kinds of jobs', the income is usually too low to cater for them and their family. Poverty is not your friend. PLAN.

SEVEN

Actualization

Photo by Kevin Bhagat on Unsplash

Actualization entails bringing your set goal into reality by applying appropriate action. It means after studying the course or acquiring the skill you have chosen based on your talent, ability, and interest, you must exercise what you have studied to achieve your set goal.

Actualization answers the question: How am I going to use or exercise what I have learned? Many graduates of today cannot practice the course they have studied because they never really got the nitty-gritty of the course. They may have studied that course because of their friends, or the course was proposed to them by their parents or even offered to them by the institution. I said the institution because many undergraduates in the Universities/Polytechnics/Colleges of Education are not studying the course they originally intended. Instead, they are given another course offered by the institution to them as an alternative because they could not meet up with the institution's requirement or due to other factors. The issue here is, if they do not develop an interest in the course given to them, it will affect them adversely. They will not be able to utilize/apply what they studied because they never had an interest in the course/profession.

My dear reader, my advice to you is that you should go for a course that you have an interest in. If you are offered a course and you think you can do it, then develop an interest in it, put in the effort and you will succeed by the grace of God. If at the end of your B.sc, HND, NCE and so on, you cannot practice what you have studied, then, you are not better than those who are seeking admission; you should be able to practice what you have studied. A lawyer that cannot defend a case in the law court is not a lawyer but has wasted his/her time in studying that course. An accountant that cannot prepare income and expenditure accounts of a non-profit organization has also wasted his/her time in studying accounting.

Consider this short story.

Many years ago, I interviewed a young graduate who wanted to teach in the school I worked at then. He was asked to go into the class and teach the SSS 1 students Accounting (Year 11 in the UK). He was to prepare a final account for a company. Disappointingly, he could not perform. The students were the ones teaching him instead. He could not apply the knowledge he had gotten from his four-year discipline in the university. Many graduates are in this category. They cannot actualize their dream just because they went for a course they don't have interest in.

Actualization involves:

- Ensuring you are well acquainted with what you studied.
- Keeping your mind on your goal.
- Applying what you have studied appropriately, and
- Realizing your goal(s).

EIGHT

Seek Advice

Photo by LinkedIn Sales Navigator on Unsplash

D ear reader, it is very paramount that you seek
advice from a career counsellor or one that
knows about choosing a career and/or you read a

book(s) on career. You may visit the internet to get information about courses you can study that will give the maximum satisfaction you desire. Some secondary schools have career counsellors. If you are a secondary school student, you could meet them to guide you in choosing a career.

Some students make counsellors of their school friends or age mates. This may not be outrightly wrong, but your friend does not have enough information/experience like a person who has been through the university system, has a steady career going well for him or her, and has knowledge and experiences having dealt with people in helping them make the right career choices. Also, someone with the knowledge or experiences related to the field you are interested in can help in guiding you. He or she would be able to give you adequate information that you need before going for the course.

Do not rely on your understanding; move closer to those who have excelled in their respective careers and get advice on how you too can excel in your career. Attend summits, career seminars and so on; get enlightened on choosing a career. You are not too young to do this. No price can be too much to get the best in the right way.

NINE

What to Do When the Situation Is Beyond Your Control

Photo by Evan Dennis on Unsplash

Despite knowing exactly what you want for your life and being ready to pursue it, we understand that some situations and circumstances could be beyond your control, or that have placed limitations on you. Some of these are family decisions (especially when your family is the dictator type), the imposition of another course option on you by the institution, lack of financial resources, etc.

In a situation where your family imposes their choice on you, if you cannot stand your ground based on your family background or threats to withdraw their resources from your education, you might need to seek scholarship opportunities, speak with a respectable person whom you believe your family would listen to, or seek the sponsorship of an elder who is willing to support your education without strings attached (do not accept ridiculous demands from this individual in question; walk away if he or she makes any). Should all efforts prove abortive, you might need to stick with what your family wants in the meantime. As soon as you can get support, or when you eventually round off with the course, you can switch to your original intention--the one that suits your career choice.

In situations where it is the institution that imposes another discipline contrary to your preference(s), you can re-apply or go ahead with the course for the first year, and then, apply for a switch to your chosen discipline ahead of the second year. Another option is to advance your studies after your university/polytechnic/College of Education degree. That is, you can opt for postgraduate school (Post Graduate Diploma, Masters, etc.) in your area of interest or at least, something close to it.

When a lack of financial resources is the limitation, try scholarship or sponsorship options. Also, you can learn a skill or get a job, raise the funds needed, and then, get yourself enrolled in the right institution. If your career choice is a hands-on skill, you can enrol in less costly monotechnics or training centres to build your skill even before you can purchase a higher and more recognised degree. Another option is to seek an apprenticeship in the meantime till you can sponsor your education.

This chapter cannot end without addressing a specific category, and that is young women who, due to tradition or financial constraints, were married early and have been unable to chase their dreams. If you fall into this category, note this: your dreams are valid. You have a potential which you must not allow to die. Look within you and identify your passion, interest and ability. Then, begin to work towards it.

If you lack support from your family, get a small job or get involved in a trade and raise the necessary resources for you to sponsor your education. Keep your goal and future in mind when doing this. You don't have to reveal this to anyone. Just stay focused until you get there. It is possible if you set your mind to it.

In other cases that are not mentioned, seek counsel from the right sources and stay guided. You can achieve your career dreams no matter what.

TEN

Relevance to Contemporary Age

Photo by Domenico Loia on Unsplash

The world today is changing very fast. New ideas and developments come in split seconds. Some years ago we were in the JET AGE.

Later on, we advanced to the COMPUTER AGE. Now, we are in the age of ARTIFICIAL INTELLIGENCE (AI). In essence, you must be acquainted with the times and seasons. Whichever course you want to study, it should be relevant to today's world so that you can remain relevant.

For instance, there was a time in Nigeria when people wanted to be typists. There was also another time when people wanted to be letter writers for the illiterates and the aged. And another when people aspired to be postmen. Today, those career aspirations have long disappeared because of technology and a continuous increase in knowledge and education. People have moved on to newer and more modern career aspirations that fall in line with the ever-changing and advancing world.

Some careers remain relevant till date. Teaching and healthcare careers are examples. There is an ever-growing demand for people in these professions due to the increase in knowledge and the need to impart them into the upcoming generation, as well as the discoveries of newer diseases plus the growing rate at which people fall ill these days. What about the information and communication sector, ICT and

Journalism? These careers become more and more relevant as time flies.

Note, however, that as relevant as they are, the method in which such careers, as well as others, operate keeps developing and advancing. Take a cue from Journalism. Once upon a time, journalists simply spoke Queen's English and read the daily reports from paper to their viewers via radio and television. But today, a journalist needs more than Queen's English. TV reporters barely read from papers these days but more from teleprompters and have to learn to read with the speed of the prompter. They also have to know more than just writing good reports, voicing and broadcasting them but also how to shoot and edit. It's called One Man Band Reporting--Multi-media Journalism (MMJ).

The same applies to other careers. They are not the same as they used to be but now operate differently and according to modern standards. So, if your career is still relevant today, you have to gain the knowledge and skills that will give you an edge in today's world.

Finally, it is pertinent to mention that there are also careers and professions that were considered irrelevant or non-existent in time past, which today, is now a 'hot cake' in society. An artist, a decade ago in Nigeria, was considered as one who had wasted his/her father's resources in training him/her with a good education. In 2021, can we say the same of an artist? How about a photographer? They were considered poor. The profession was one in which people only took up just to survive but today, the huge developments and advancements that have taken place in the world of photography are mind blowing. A photographer can now conveniently be a celebrity based on his/her expertise. There was no profession as ghostwriting in time past. As at then, to be seen as the author of a book, you have to have spent time, ink, energy, physical and mental effort in putting words to paper, and then, submit to a publisher who would, first, approve it before publishing and distributing your books to the populace. But all that has changed. You can now conveniently pay a professional writer to help modify your ideas into a book. The ghostwriter does the job of re-arranging your ideas, writing them into a book-length manuscript and sometimes, editing the manuscript for you. When it is published, you have your name on it as the author. Nearly every celebrity these days uses ghostwriters for their books.

Whatever you choose to be, ensure it is relevant to the age you are in, gain the knowledge, and develop the skills that will put you in command in your field.

About the Author

Olushola Adeborode, Kolawole is simply an exceptional and outstanding leader. He studied Economics at Olabisi Onabanjo University, Ago-Iwoye and later proceeded to Heriot-Watt University, Scotland, the UK where he bagged a Master's Degrees in Logistics and Supply Chain Management. He holds a PhD in Operations and Supply Chain Management at the University of Bradford.

He is a member of local and international professional bodies which include; Nigeria Institute of Management (Chartered), Chartered Institute of Logistics and Transport (UK), Council of Supply Chain Management Professionals (USA), Chartered Institute of Procurement and Supply (CIPS), UK among others.

Olushola is an award winner both at the state and national level which was bestowed upon him by the then Zamfara State Governor, Alhaji Mamuda Shinkafi, and the Nigerian President, Goodluck Ebele Jonathan, (GCFR), for his selfless service during his one-year mandatory service to his fatherland. He is the Founder/CEO of The King's Palace Schools, Lagos/Ogun, Nigeria. He is also the founder of OAK Foundation, a charity organisation aimed at supporting indigent students, widows and fatherless in Africa. He is also the CEO of a UK based company, New Touch Int. Ltd, UK. Dr. Olushola currently lectures and supervise research students at the following universities:

- University of Bradford
- Royal Holloway University
- Buckingham New University
- University of Essex (Online)

He is a member of Board of Trustees of different organisations both home and abroad. He loves God passionately.

Printed in Great Britain
by Amazon

73428141R00047